T0150661

TODD SWIFT

Opening Hours

NEW POEMS

∞ MAIDA VALE PUBLISHING

ANY SALES PROFITS FOR THIS BOOK
ARE TO GO TO ALEX, THE AUTHOR'S GODSON,
WHO IS ON THE AUTISM SPECTRUM

First published in 2021
by Maida Vale Publishing Ltd
Suite 333, 19-21 Crawford Street
Marylebone, London W1H 1PJ
United Kingdom

Typeset with artwork and graphic design by Edwin Smet

ISBN 978-1-913606-53-4

WWW.EYEWEARPUBLISHING.COM

THANK YOU TO THE DESIGN MASTER
AND BEAUTIFUL ARTIST
MY FRIEND, EDWIN SMET

TABLE OF CONTENTS

8   BRIEF INTRODUCTION

11 FIVE HALF-SONNETS, POEM FOR JOHN KEATS COMPOSED
        EXACTLY 200 YEARS AFTER HIS DEATH, IN LONDON
13 ROLLING, ROLLING
15 THE AMBULANCE
17 NOVEMBER 2020
19 LOCKDOWN 2
21 FOR PIERRE LAPORTE
25 ON READING A SECOND-HAND BOOK, 1959
27 SUNLIGHT IN THE WORLD
29 THE DARK
31 PERRY MASON
32 MR SMITH GOES HOME TO NOTHING
34 MUSK BEATS BEZOS TO THE TOP
36 NATURE STOLE FATHERING FROM ME
37 A QUEBEC FARMHOUSE IN SUMMER
40 POETIC FRAGMENTS COMPOSED ON IPHONE, 2020
46 CHILL, CHILL
47 POEM WITH MOSTLY ONE RHYME SCHEME
48 THAT BEST OF YEARS
50 A CHILD'S CHRISTMAS IN QUEBEC
53 NEW GOLD DREAM, 21, 22, 23, 24...
55 FOR THE EASTER OF 2021, IT MAY BE
58 THE IDYLLS OF THE FOOL – 5 SONNETS AND A CODA
61 NEW SPRING POEM IN 33 COUPLETS
64 'THIS IS THE POEM'
66 THE POST OFFICE
70 BORN TO BE WILD
75 FOR SUETONIUS
76 CATHY'S CLOWN
78 55 (X 2)

84 BIO NOTE

BRIEF INTRODUCTION

This is a collection of my more recent, unpublished poems. It is an unofficial sequel to last year's *Spring In Name Only*. I'd hope the poems were clever, well-made or stylish enough to entertain, or alarm, or move – all three together, ideally. Poems are like prayers in a not entirely good religion. Poems are not medicine, but they may be pills. How you take them is which den you lie in.

I will make no apologies for the ideas and characters you may find within these pages – these lyrics and narratives are entirely fictional, even when based on personal experience. They may amplify or embody, or perform, aspects of my selves, but they are better enjoyed or received as symbolic of various ways of speaking out.

The main paradigm of my work, however modified by post-modernity, has been that of the ever-changing canon that Eliot posited. These poems are in delirious dialogue with previous poems, they speak to the dead, and one day will be dead themselves, to be spoken to in their turn, one hopes.

There has been a terrible pandemic, but somehow, we carried on, and the light came back into the world, very slowly, as the vaccinations seemed to be pushing lives back from a very real if invisible brink. It was all very tiring, strange, frightening, sometimes motivating, often deeply depressing and sad, and maybe, a way to find resilience.

I suppose this has been a time to think of the deadly baton, gun and contagion, the fragile, the less-so – what ends, what endures – the scientific, the mysterious, the numinous, the luminous, death, love, lust, books, friends, brothers, mothers, others, masks, masques, TV, movies, music, food, sleep, walks, cats, fear, hope, and how the seasons are more than background for a play, but sometimes the stage itself.

April 26 2021, Maida Vale, London, England

Note: fellow poets Christopher Jackson and Alex Wylie offered kind comment on some of these poems, which encouraged me to publish them.

'Closer together...
and make it all worthwhile'

– The Box

FIVE HALF-SONNETS, POEM FOR JOHN KEATS COMPOSED EXACTLY 200 YEARS AFTER HIS DEATH, IN LONDON

Now at the hour when most do sleep
I read out of Norton poems by Keats
unable to find drowsiness or Lethe
here where truth leads youth's beauty
to see gold dominions invisibly deep;
long have I aimed at the steep reaches
of polar austerity where few explore

without some keen perversity keening
to them to seek ice citadels so purely
formed as jewels by a crafty godhead
whose breath forms crystals of snow
as poets breathe sonnets from souls;
no difference but climate and geography
between those who go into wilderness

to become a knower of unsaid things
and my kind grown capable in astute
cunning able to discover newly made
kingdoms, fiery tropical or deadly
frozen – further their furred bearing
princesses, scholars, rascals, kings,
leaning on marble as if for posterity

unwise to their being merely creatures
fictioned in London with a sleeping
brain, aware of the night's long abysms
that wake a maker to start up again
to light a taper casting lumination
scattering shadows like leaves playing
in a sonnet ripe with autumn dread

but also fecund with gaudy taverns
those bright legumes farmers bring
golden yellows from treasure harvesting
as if rich vines themselves were mined,
carved from mountains as if surgery
had cut away soft earth to expose
how mind is burning dark, darkly burning.

FEBRUARY 2021

ROLLING, ROLLING

There was a painting, in a small oval frame
In my grandmother's house, of a sailing ship

Crossing the ocean, and I can't remember
The waves, but there was also another

Frame, a photo, of a boy in a silly suit,
Who wasn't her, but her father, I think,

And they were on the kitchen wall, right by
Where she once dropped me when

I was little, so my teeth cut through
My lower lip, and I needed stitches,

And that still perceptibly shows, barely,
And they'd drink tea and have bacon sandwiches

Slathered with HP sauce, when I was four
Or five, and they talked about the old country,

Meaning Ireland, or my grandfather's London,
This was in Montreal by the way, actually

My Uncle's house but he let her live there,
Because my grandfather had died on a golf course

Under a tree, during a storm, where he taught
The game to wealthier men, of heart failure,

I would look at the painting and imagine waves,
Dark rolling dark waves, and how cold

How terrifically deep cold and lonely
The waves were, and how lonely the sailing was,

And I'd feel a chill run through me, that felt like
A future, where I would have travelled far

From the warmth, and hilarity of those occasions,
To a place of dark waves and rolling dark waves

On top of dark waves, and it felt like England,
I thought that is what England would be like, then.

NOVEMBER 2020

THE AMBULANCE

I'd tend to draw it out
As something pregnant, freighted,
A thing that lodges in the heart

When seen, a bad luck image
That hurts the eye; meaning
Nothing ever very good, usually

Worse than that. Many moving vehicles
Carry ideas in their stride, ambulances
Tend to show more than they hide,

Flashing their bright yellow jackets
Of urgent care, implying pain.
You don't fix what isn't broken,

They say, as they speed, make way
For someone else's trouble, yours
Can wait. We duly step aside, to see

Another world's quickly departing emergencies.
But today, down the hall, where my window is,
An office now, jerry-built for Covid-times,

Stacked high with papers, books and debts
It's hard to pay when sales are down,
And books stamped non-essential, hardly,

It slipped a blue swift bird of lights, velocity,
Across my line of sight like a beautiful apprehension
That the natural world, and the world we save,

Are, if not one, then almost the same, and this bird
I glimpsed, fleeting as any arrow shot through woods,
Was branching its own tree as it fled down

Streets to hit some target where they lay, to bury
Deep into the moment a stop or start, carefully
Like any flying creature lands, who also owns the air.

NOVEMBER 2020

Sometimes with elections
They get so exciting
We all forget we'll die.
There we are, riled up,
Jeering or elated,
Having lifted some stranger
Into temporary powers,
Like building a kite from red paper.
It isn't fake. Artifice
Doesn't pulse or quake quite like this.
This popcorn puke razzmatazz
Is life, this is what stinger it stings with:

Ignorant events, trombones, hot cries
In the angry morning.
Don't fret at earthly delight.
Soon a new candidate will rise.
Campaign volunteers jig under balloons
Drifting down like war-ash.
Bunting in barns, banners, betrayal,
All shifting, afterwards, gathering
Some place only diligent post-Dillinger FBI
Archivists care to find, in files marked Y
For Yore. To say it's functionless is a lie –
It mattered when it did, to us, in the Then.

Time's like a ballot box, empty, then filled
Importantly, then counted out then taken away,
Then empty all over again, for a while.

It's annoyingly infinite, the ways to describe
What we shed by having to change daily,
Importance is a thing with sides
That constantly skew sideways, open
To an eternity that has no clear definitions.
Things get going, go useless, grow new planks.
Those ships with high white sails going fast
Are now autumn trees, replicas for bored tours,
Each one a losing victory, standing to be corrected.

LOCKDOWN 2

Like the bad old days, but over again,
Like it had to happen, but always to you,
Like the retrograde mission, but not to Mars,

Like déjà vu, but the French went first,
Like it could have been prevented, but not,
Like worst foot forward, never best thought.

Like a falling milk glass, but before the tears,
Like running away, but after worst fears,
Like an explosion at work, but this time from home,

Like a failure of nerve, but one that went halfway,
Like never enough, but about too far,
Like over too soon, but longer than the year.

Like transparently stupid, but never noticeably clear,
Like a rhyme that won't click, but it must somehow,
Like arms around the weak, but they are on their own,

Like keep the wolves from the door, but not the care home,
Like we are all in this together, but some of us have cars,
Like it is almost over, but the box set's higher than the moon.

Like a nightmare on Downing Street, but closer still,
Like a necessary evil, but not everyone seems essential,
Like a sharp end of the wedge, but a broken pencil,

Like a mask to save lives, but the lives are losing,
Like a moral duty, but the amoral exact the cost,
Like a time that is slowly revolting, but it is rotten too.

Like I think I am going edgy, but there's no room left,
Like the world's gone off its axis, but also bereft,
Like the herd driven by the blind, but we're clear-eyed,

Like a vehicle roaring off a cliff, but we are inside,
Like a bad past mistake in history, but it is about now,
Like I wish I'd left instead, but it's past way too late to go.

NOVEMBER 2020

FOR PIERRE LAPORTE
Murdered 50 years ago

Writing, what does it do for you?
And in another official language,
Whose form is power, or its display,
Or the way that power ebbs, or flows.
I knew you, back when you were less

Than murdered, or more than a way
To mention terror. Poets have taught
That what we say can go low, or higher,
Slow down the subtleties of horror,
Or defer or defray the impacts.

Tact and tension, inches of pressure.
It was in October, and I was four.
A father, you played on your front lawn
With your family, throwing a ball
Around in the early autumn air.

Leaves were goldening; the great river
Was only feet or metres away; bucolic
Is not quite correct, but closer than a lie.
Fiction says I was there; the actuality is
I was nearby, with my own father,

At our own play; but the same avenue,
Putney (their house on the higher corner)
On the South Shore. This took place
In varying languages, French for the minister
Of the government, Anglo-talk for me

And my dad, Tom. They took him that day.
When he was found, days later, in the car,
They thought him the English diplomat, instead.
The French Quebecer could not even be identified
At first when dead. Soon, he was announced

As gone. No one, not even now, can say,
In any dialect or fashion, whatever linguistic
Method you'd like to try, how the death-grip
Came to be applied, that rendered him a fact
You can look up online. Something beyond playing

And Thanksgiving, the smell of burnt leaves in air.
Far past pathos, nostalgic reckonings, or desire
For vengeance, or recollection; fifty years
Does havoc to the remnant brain; time blows
The candles out, and not to state the obvious, but,

Not for a birthday; bathos, or restraint, both go
To an articulation unasked for. And when did poems
Last have anything to do with Montreal, really?
And who even, these deceptively ludicrous, tough hours,
Turns to A.M. Klein, our maestro of the international

Interleaving of lingos, from Joyce's Riverrun to Iago's?
Poems gets uncounted like archipelagos contain
Flotsam, jetsam, the insane tortoise or two; chaos
And disorder remain the librarian in the canon, truthfully.
I've found, amidst researches in vast libraries, hermetic,

Urbane, with coffee shops for hearts, and gift shops
For brains, lost plunder buried in plain sight, on paper.
Piratical poesy that no one under the sun now bothers

To covet or adore. I mean, and here the I is genuinely
Me trying to speak to you, if you are there, not just

A closed link or cover, page on page on page of smothering,
He was strangled on his chain, a crucifix around his throat,
Too perfect an image to be invented for aesthetic pleasure.
Crumpled, or merely rammed somehow into the boot, the trunk,
And abandoned, to be found, like any poem or useless treasure

Made of a fool's errand; was it manslaughter or cold-blooded,
Or some accidental manoeuvre in-between? Emblematic,
Of the measures to be taken, the lost innocence of the times,
And it framed, your death, that death, his death, my father's
Reactions, ever afterwards; and so, I suppose, mine; how he'd

Never sleep well again, wake at night, in terror, to check
The doors, the windows, our beds; thinking someone was coming.
And they had come, and they had taken, from Cross, the Brit attaché,
To Laporte, hung on his cross, in Paul Rose's vehicle.
I am the way, the door, too neat by half

For any cenotaph, the names that drag us forward, tug back.
Half a century and the actors are removed from recognition.
Not that any of us are, or were, genuinely acting, or actors,
Despite Shakespeare saying so. I read yesterday, this in twenty-twenty,
That even the Bard is under siege, interrogated, held to account

For his politics, his views. No sacred texts then, anymore, if ever,
And history is like a fleuve, or a veuve, a widow or shadow, a going.
Nothing is a lot of water to unload and sift; my gifts were startled
Into fluency at four by your amazing murder, that captured my family,
Our imagination, that shaped, from mere opinion, hardened ideas,

On identities, and friction. I've had to have your massacre with me
Daily like a nightmare burial, like a meal, or the anxiety it invoked.
The war of fear that stormed my house, also, down the same street.
And if we ever meet, may I ask you for a simplistic favour, if ideal?
Don't go out to play, Pierre, in October; stay indoors, to heal us all.

OCTOBER 2020

ON READING A SECOND-HAND BOOK, 1959

I have done evil things,
Evil things were done to me.
We speak in evil when we try
To explicate our reasons to be free.
It is evil that cries when they weep.
We should open channels to bring across
Our thoughts of evil, to the mountain kings.

The good we did was accidental.
The rest was evil, from sun to star.
It is evil to have loved and been brutal,
Evil to want what law tends to bar.
History is evil, written by a crime
Too monumental to stop or have
To apologise, to all who died

Why even when we tried, sometimes,
To holster devils, more often, we just lied.
All evil is in evil, streaking out to God.
God trembles at the wound, must recoil.
It is essential to seek compromise, before
The rot in the canopy outstays the fragrant hour.
I mean, accept the evil, in all creatures,

From hoopoe to zebra, elephant to gazelle,
As their mortal pulse – grazer or hunter,
All crouched or crouching, speeding or most still,
Calm in predestined dying or eating off the same kill.
It isn't odd out in the open or in the bush, to see
How each creation wills to crawl about the bottom
Of a scorched, eluvial crater or heart-stained flood.

It does no good to debate a savage carnivore,
Condemn the Equator or execute Victoria Falls.
We came to this world, superior, like our creator,
To do evil, without exception, since we could.
This is life, learn to see the moral in epigrams,
Camps, wired lanes. They speak most plainly
Who carry carbines and never aim to explain.

SUNLIGHT IN THE WORLD

Strict observation does no good
Unless you trust the reporter,
Will my lozenge or gum stopper of light

Improve your own eyesight?
What did poetry think it was bringing
When it yoked imagery together

Like blind Milton's slaves?
The poor violated things forced
To do labour they were never born for.

The poet's a violent creator, thinking
An art willed by passion, drawn
From a god or more, is divine,

If only barely, and unwell.
It smacks of colonies, interventions,
Doing unto others what they don't want.

Still, I say I see a new way to see,
Then flaunt an odd description,
As if becoming evolution speeding.

It's a trick, and time is up, it's been
Seen through. Poems are cinematic
Before the new technology came along.

Song sings better, fairer, more true.
Science works harder to prove.
The sun this September sets a mood

Both still and promising. It holds
A brief interlude, before the locking
To return. The light doesn't burn

Like it could. It behaves. It plays
Like a mild lover, at the end of loving.
The garden is a tousled bed,

And all the furious making out now
Lays suspended over the world
Like a nail gun had penetrated my head.

THE DARK

The dark is rising, but it always has
Been an upstart, just because
That's what darkness does.
We have the horizon to focus on,

That way the high Beaufort
Won't render us sick, again.
Grip your ice pick, prepare
To wrestle on the ice. Fittest

Survive, the rest get locked down
In the sinking feeling part of town.
Shoulder your Winchester,
We all require level action now,

Now that lever-repeating guns
Are everywhere. Smell the cinders
Blocking the daily air. Winter arrives
Like the apologetic ticket collector

Who knows you don't carry one,
Will have to nudge you off the train.
Let's face it, you'll hold on,
Somehow, tethered to the caboose,

With a leather noose. Reveal
Your shining scalpels, doctors
Of the new strange constraints,
Begin to cut and tear at what's wrong;

It's never light, and the money's gone,
But there's more of us than them,
And we can sort of hum Shelley's songs.
Strap those masques on, Anarchies!

PERRY MASON

Unlocked down, and I am thinking Indochine,
Despite its Orientalist name, is the best band EVER,
Which will be news to my friends, out there,
If they even care, but I am once again in euphoric
Cartwheels, a feeling, such as those are, inside,
That all is incredibly escaped, we made it through,
Not true, if you count the many war dead all told,
If you count this as a war, if you consider it at all.
Prestige *Perry Mason* is on, and is very gruesome,
Like the *Andalusian Dog*, lots of eye cruelty,
I am simply happy to be listening to French pop.
Dostoyevsky similarly got gripped at roulette.
I love my pet, love my way of standing, my haircut.
The day, the week, the month, the year, out of its rut.

JULY 2020

MR SMITH GOES HOME TO NOTHING

He packs his box in another box,
Adjusts his mask over his other mask,
And hails a taxi to take him to his car;
It's not far to his secret identity, as Mr Jones;
Scan the bones, he's the same under the mac.
He doesn't think back to the start of the race,
He's run it over in his mind before, he fell
Before the wire, and anyway, that was ages
Away in the first book. He thinks his life
Is a trilogy, that no one has published yet.
Always too late to sign up for that gym class;
He ends up at the two addresses, side by side;
One where he doesn't live, the other where
He doesn't hide. In neither can he fully abide
The way fur grows on his back and under his nose.
He's a human, he guesses, in the double mirror,
No valet to his heroes. In one version
He was castrated in Istanbul; in the latter,
His was the harem. Neither appears to exist
In Telford, where he tells himself he is at rest
Before his bodies snap into action. He's a sex
Pistol, a whipcrack, a set of barbells for girls,
Pink. He's objectified, despite trying to split
Into the man emerging from the mist, the man
Entering the raincloud. It's not about being proud,
But he's in control of your mind. He has a skin
That lies under his skin; he has a favour to ask
Of your life that involves a memory from boyhood.
The day he saw her, all in yellow, beneath the bus,
With the red and white fuss, on the floor.

He wants to go to there, and a bit before.
You're the reason he's on this app. He's
The brother you never knew you needed to have.
He has a van on lease with a thousand miles left.
His name is double-barrelled. He's also in Spain.
Some powers are unexplained, they just flood
The plains like power does. He knows you.
It's a handful having to exist in stages, a rocket
That will break apart, one by one, to get farther out;
He's on the way, he's reaching your remote door.
Firing aspects of your fate are interlocking now.

MUSK BEATS BEZOS TO THE TOP

My father despised
Suits, wore them every day for 35 years
Of service, got applause and a watch
On his last day, was deflated, if sober;
They once measured his desk, concluded,
The nabobs, it was a centimetre too big
For his position's ranking, on a scale
Of authority measured first at MIT.
There isn't an ounce or degree
That's not been tested by some mind
Advanced by a machine or three;
So I went about my work with integrity
Tempered by a temperament best described
As a bust-up in a boxing club;
Irish partly, insecure, small-town boy
In the Big City, a poet with sensitivities;
When what is called for in a company
Is a robot who plays golf and has an MBA;
The disruptors tend to be super-funded geeks
With less Latin than Greek, and less poetry;
Their idea of creation is to destroy bricks,
Mortar, main streets, whole ways of doing
Things; centuries fall like English wickets
During a hot test under the Silicon bowlers;
Defeated prime ministers go to Lord's,
Reassured by a pace that softens doom
To a quiet day growing gently older;
The speed of money-making is not directed
To compassion, empathy or slim volumes;
They say poetry sells well, but they would;
Compared to gold, guns and lies, not so much.

In a blatant, spinning, populist world,
All my aims were skewed, utterly.
It's my fault I drowned, in the sense
I went for a swim in the Thames;
Took a bath on the high-risk shoals
Of publishing; it is audible, the disdain
The eventual horizon forecasts for the time
That may remain; we're rising to a heat-death
That makes insane scientist ray-guns
Look benign; look out for your coastlines,
I am a witness to full frontal
Decline, to be determined by the rabble
Of stages of murderous stupidity rebranded
As rebooting and velocity. They realign
The powers that are to the powers that will be;
It's a new ancestry being landed on shores of ingenuity;
And the majority will be sold a blank bill of goods

Not good in the least; so it always was, since PT
Barnum's swaggering; but then they traded in tents,
And those big tops caught fire or swept away in Kansas;
Whereas now the distant cloud-based billionaires
Advance in a sort of gilded impermeability, rude
To the past, and daring to moon-shot to Mars, beyond,
So that ice never settles for long on any skater's pond;
Break apart what you can, raise the pick, bring it down;
The nations are splintering, and we're Atlantis-sunk
Except for the immortals who soon will commute
Their corporeal templates to a never-ending life sentence;
A percentile who designed a world for their own smart kind,
While the turbulent rest of us, workers, makers, feelers,
Get post-human make-overs, stifled in a steel carapace;
Scuttling over dusty, cold, dull surfaces of planetoids
To mine minerals for the great industries in the void.

NATURE STOLE FATHERING FROM ME

before I was made;
seedless like a special
grape, the doctor said;
the total pain took
on my limited identity;
the boat my body shook
with the fact's indignity.
Now I am father to books,
and cats, the day,
the air, fire and water too.
I am a universal father
knowing bonds unbind
but love decided is full true.
My body failed, my soul refused
to be seen as useless or defused.
It grew beyond mere need
to free Adam and Eve,
for the unmaking few supersede
the merely created tree.

A QUEBEC FARMHOUSE IN SUMMER

I have it in my head
But the sun brings it out
Summer in the Eastern
Townships, evocative place name
For the settled woodlands, farms
Of Quebec closest to the Americans,

Their brutal border; the loyal came
Over, when nation broke from empire;
But there's no history for me but grandparents,
Trees, books, and heat, reading Lampman
Near the hay, the cornfields, the pond;
That quaint rhymer, who knew

How to sound like a British poet,
Then threw a bit more of Canada in,
Like frogs, and days of shocking light –
A furnace he'd called it, Ontario
Out of winter into the open months,
The blazing upturning glory of provincial weather;

In the heather, near the croquet lawn, I sit
With tea and sandwiches, and caravans
Of books, ignoring the dumbass games
My cousins rope the rest into, the violence
Of being young near a forest in July;
There's no reason to relate these events;

No hate or holding back because of skin or birth,
Except my language was policed by the state,
And like all children, I'd seen past innocence
And could relate to the wolves we'd hear
Some late hours, by the window looking out
Onto calm pastures, unsettling depths of firs;

What occurs to me now, is, this was entitled
Terror, my misborn anxieties, the familial disjointedness
A white empire of tedious safeties that only
Seemed spoiled by drink, rage and incestuous acts;
In retrospect, the sun was hot, I survived, to live more,
To write self-interested lyrics of a land

No one has interest in, except the dethroned,
The indigenous who have been overthrown
By successions of invaders gauche as greed;
That grabbing also policed; the language anxieties
In my province have to come from knowing
The root tongue was never francophone, or Anglo,

There were others in the forests besides the beasts;
But in my time, at fourteen, it was ugly puberty,
Lonesome dithering, plunging into writing, self-lust,
And a growing overall miscast apprehension of mistrust;
But it was beautiful, and contained, and, if not
Unmolested, then mainly unquestioned, our right

To loll afternoons to take our time with English literature,
To plan for a future, that, then, appeared uncontested.
How wrong it was to see it that way, any way,
To think seeing back to my childhood or teen years
Has value or heft at all, except as warning or apology.
I was born privileged even in my aristocratic debts;

Whatever was done to me was done elsewhere, worse,
I must ride now across my estates to make repairs,
Until the end of all conquest, when knighthoods end.
But that, of course, is ridiculous, overstated, false.
I've got no horse, can barely scrape together two kopeks;
Poems are vain carriers of recompense. I'll try to rewrite.

POETIC FRAGMENTS COMPOSED ON IPHONE, 2020

afraid for what is coming afraid for what has come afraid for what we will do afraid for what has never been done afraid of my own shade afraid of the improper glade afraid of The Spain rate afraid of the state of our wretched state afraid to go to stay afraid to game the stain of play or end this only way.

I try to feel more than feeling can / think over what thinking scans / the wave has wings of water in its mouth / Venice sinks to ask for lurid truth / this is the all too much of days / spanning cankers too sore to praise / the supreme lie God is art to love us whole / in an age of artless hatreds Homer full / throw down vain bows, try to endure / in toppled Troy devoid of tragic cure.

impossible not to be thankful as me this year of worst outcomes for so many; I am alive gratefully; as are others I know; virus of knowledge we learn from your spread; learn a distant thanksgiving, ironic; no, sincere how I want to draw near to a flame I can't survive; thankful fewer than possible are currently dead, knowing burning will arrive also, maybe. Yes.

A poem can do anything but one thing it should try to do is be the poem that comes after all the earlier ones, with that full weight and that full permission in that rich understanding. It should be a good listener and a better speaker and a better Jazz player and it should if it wants to play off all the other beats and notes and echoes and day-trips and blind alleys and byways and highways and passions of all of poetry from the start of the world. It should blow its horn in the proud company of greats, in humble companionship and generous accompaniment.

Between nothing and something
I'll take either. Sleep or heaven;
hell is too complicated, seems
overkill.

Only a hoarder wants to outlast Kondo; letting go of all the mind
clutter, ego files is what owning a PC prepares us for – junking
folders; sad not to do more; but only gluttons eat four desserts
which is like living much longer.

It's a concert, it ends, you exit.

Even Elvis left the building. Even the big lady has to sing. It won't
not happen, like tomorrow, rain.

At least everyone gets the same
ultra-blank or eternity-surprise,
and unlike birth it has no pain.
Try to avoid it long as you can –
live as if the best to hope for
is unending (until sun-ends) fame.

the young are different finally than the old, they have they think
more time to use, but also less world each day to lose; they worry
slowly, move with reckless care; their angers are infinite, their
patience rare; they hate more, more often than I recall at their
stage; age is a moving target; all slip along like a pickpocket hoping
not to be caught; feel September on my tongue; a cold shiver
sliding between careful bones; this worst year no longer young,
each shoulders their share of an adding burden, understands the
weight unseen.

consider the new met lovers waiting for a vaccine to kiss as if 2021 was their wedding horizon on which to sail a hopeful bed meanwhile aching for lips to find what Keats knew never happens on an ideal ancient vase except by human flaws: time delays even as it flows to impale desire on a true law of things – beauty rarely stays like an army burning as it goes, taking needfully I am not in the book the book ker-chug ker-chug that all the young ladies and gentlecads love they love ker-puff ker-puff so my bankbooks are rough so rough dear boys oh dear so my diary is dreary in fear oh fear no not in their books their books my dear for fear I'd be spotted like the best lost glove at last so best so loved!

I have been telling you I am a genius for so long now even I am tired of the ruckus but I know since my soul is neatly folded between the pages of German poets who owned passionate revolvers and were sickly; my aches are not comical but actual and only in English is meaning chafed so by irony it is impossible to sing with august pain do a little less each day dip into the abyss of gentle resignation including no sweets or bread so you grow tiny and eventually are 19th century in size miniature but still vitally important to a few historians but mind you don't get over your head in disputes since war is the next station.

I am the man in the garden who carries his black indoors six kilogram four year old best friend cat with him back and forth every evening lifting his chap into low leaves and close to roses so his soft versatile associate can sniff what is above his usual reach except when leaping and yes we are so happy very within our own lodgings called appreciation in these slightest motions.

We are all tired of washing our hands in this sectioned world and by we, I mean everybody; speaking globally is now within my radius. This power is So, my futile gesture of an us when I am now less even than a me. Halved by distance I come across this divisive space to see my own face masked in the mirror that was your kiss. Narcissus herself would shiver at the mess. It's tiredness, this tiring endless distress masquerading as medical calamity. To be plain, we all want out into what comes next.

This has nothing to do with me
which is why it does;
like in a prison the bars make
prisoners, but there's more;
nothing I do or say seems
to alter the problem when
what I do or say is the problem;
if the house is rotten tear down
the house then; stepping aside
is not going to cut it; got to cut in
to the skin and tear away

that mark that marks what dreams get made to stay; not going to be easy but hard tries though trying's not enough now; you're the field or the plough.

time lately has gone wild like a mirror against a mirror in a rainstorm so sliding is the very weather of the day I've come to miss my own life like it was a glove I dropped in a cinema during a fire I want to kiss strangers during a red plane crashing; dream of sleep jolt out of reality screaming for her/him/me the first man on the maroon isle of cats.

does anyone else
crave an outlet
past the sea door,
through the cobalt straits,
under the limestone gowns,
across the bridge of lies,
over the cornfed moon,
via the granite statues,
burning the taboo gates,
to finally arrive at the Nile
of whatever you want to do,
the sea red as lips,
burning with all Cleopatra's
useless ships on balmy nights?

Caligula, Don Juan, Byron,
I fear mouth watering fuss
is always folly in daylight;
freedom is what we die for
when Greece demands we fight.
Life is almost always
unbearable because
you have what you want
or almost have what you want
or don't have what you want
and unbearable because
what you want is unacceptable
or almost unacceptable
or so acceptable you say so what;

or you want something beyond
some thing, beyond wants,
even beyond becauses;
and that too is unbearable

because then you want God
or else you want the obverse
of what wanting God is –
and evil and good both ache
to attain levels above aching.

CHILL, CHILL

Chill, chill and ash grey, that cold, as if
on purpose November mornings now.
This is where misplaced things
and all those naked implications
in their difficulties
conspire – less vindictively,
they gather. It is not their fault

November disrobes all leaders
or strips the simplest stick.
Out in an unexpected waking dawn,
too early for conversations,
the sky has a dark to light allure.
I cross a mismanaged lawn, lost
in basic clutter, thinking

of some dead, a missing aspect.
Proverbial, to find here a savage cut,
its finality barely sweet,
branches, in name only, looking old.
A lie it will stay this austere:
return is hidden nature of a tree.
No leave-taking without a later leaf.

POEM WITH MOSTLY ONE RHYME SCHEME

It came upon me like a midnight clear,
Nothing circumspect about abject fear
One year I'd been barely able to cobble together
Reasons for the forward trundle among mean peers
Now the twenty-twenty experience, total weird.
We've all been here, it's that rare spectacular
You don't need eyes to see, beyond veneer
I'd gone one better, though, felt no longer mere
Me or someone other, I'd just blinked out and over
Like the plunked phone in the canal, so far, so near
Flatter than the death rate fun park rollercoaster.

I've lost, not tattletale smell, but taste for career
Spiritual renewal or nada plus plus – down, yes, doctor
But not like I'd ever known such arctic wastes before
There I was, all of a sudden framed in fur,
Goggled, with skidoo, top rifle, assisted by laser
Entirely prepped for any blizzard or ice-pick meteor
Come to stock-standstill even the sub-zero thought bizarre
As awestruck bears in their whites bowed at my feet, polar
And barking seals crowned me their king-conqueror
Of land drier colder farther lesser, much leaner drear
Ever found, by whatever strives to consider life dear.

NOVEMBER 2020

THAT BEST OF YEARS

On days like this I just want to suck on a boiled sweet
And be a boy called Roger, whose glum existence
Is about to be changed on a gloomy, grey day
At his Uncle's in the Cotswolds, when a sign
From another world, possibly Saxon, or Jute,
Breaks into the Anglican community at Christmas,
And the bronze-age sword in the drawing room
Begins to glow umber at night, as owls
Hunt voles, and a light frost lands at midnight
On the ruined chestnut trees down the lane.

It is 1970, and there are a few new anthologies
Discussing a young poet called Horace,
But otherwise, the main idea is that science
Is coming, and the future is geodesic; also,
Population is a time bomb as the covers show,
With the globe shaped like a bomb, with a fuse,
As if Africa was an anarchist in a Conrad novel.
And as Roger's Uncle has a rather large library,
Which you access via a panel hidden in the pantry,
You have read all the books about jetpacks,

The police action in Indochina, and Aleister Crowley.
It is this last tome, then the others, which you begin
To scour, that lead you to believe he is a necromancer,
Which explains the sword, plus a growing thrum
At night, coming from Farmer Brown's disused barn.
Then, the squat maid, Mrs Claxton, goes missing,
Inexplicably, and Detective Glancer appears

On the scene with his obnoxious pipe and wellies,
To investigate. It snows constantly, as in Lapland,
And when it stops, it rains like a sou'wester.

The tin mines are closed, and the hills hollowed out.
Arthur's true seat beckons, and queer signals appear.
A rabbit is found half-skinned, but in no pain.
Soon it will be the solstice, and who knows what
Could happen then? That is the sort of year
I'd like to have, to feel happening, being sixteen,
Again, in mucky weather, with religious danger
In the air, but an ultimate courage, burning within
My amulet, connecting my spirit to the Silver Lexicon,
As I was soon to learn that rum evening at the vicarage.

DECEMBER 2020

A CHILD'S CHRISTMAS IN QUEBEC

Who doesn't suddenly recall
At Christmas, a small act
That was never forgotten?
A father, drunk on his pay,
Staggering home at midnight,
No good Santa, with last-minute
Presents, including a Parker Brothers
Game, all the silly money flying

When the box breaks, the plastic cars.
A grandmother who went to all
The trouble of finding, in the department
Store hurly-burly, a vinyl record,
When all records were vinyl, Nick Gilder's
LP, because at ten years old,
That's what you wanted, and back then,
People had to actually go out

And get gifts, to bring them back,
Which was, in retrospect, which this is,
A truly remarkable, and kind thing, to do.
The collecting of webbed firewood
From the basement, mother's crab
Dip with sesame crackers, the mulled wine,
The snowstorms, the church service
With cardboard golden crowns for the wise

Men, the grape-juice for the wine for the blood.
The thud of snowballs thrown at windows,
The delivering of newspapers to widows,
The self-pleasure at reading Huysmans,
The fireplace, the stereo, the thrilling teenage glow,
Kissing your barely-girlfriend while listening
To Bing Crosby sing *let it snow, let it snow.*
This won't let go, these old tidings,

Rattling their Marley chains, they're part
And wrapped parcel of you, no one else's.
Your stash, your hoard, your piece on the board.
Monopoly is what young egos think they own.
If only, eh, you'd once upon a Christmas known,
How most of the aunties, uncles, third cousins
With their gin breathe and old-world stories,
Are further on, into this latest year, yes, ghosts;

That hoary chestnut, word of a thousand poems.
No hell roasts those long gone, go out
Into the garden, the little tree's been blown
Over, the string of lights still battery-on,
The wind's rising, the forecast is bleak, then
Bleaker still for later in the week, the branches
Look like men left dead in world war one trenches,
They soldier on as best they can, decomposing

In the mud, the green and brown merge,
There's a bewildering lack of diffusion,
Instead, a concentrated sense of dread calm,
A stillness like after an avalanche,
The darkening day lowers the bar,
The solstice is around a corner, but until

The world wheels back on its heels gratuitously
Fortunate to have a built-in swivel to the sun,

We're momentarily bee-in-the-jam in the palm
Of a giant melancholy drift to night,
The night before Christmas, when everyone's
Expectations prepare to be confused, disowned,
And the child cries for opening the wrong box,
Or complains, or an inebriate groans, licks
The reindeer's cookie plate, rises, crumbs
On his silver beard, looks around like Pilate,

To realise there is no truth, no beauty in locks,
Pulls out a key and runs pell-mell into an avenue,
Giving back to his society all that at which him
They once variously, indifferently, threw.
We see him, call the police, get on with our rums
And cola, our little review of given gains,
The tissue, and paper thrown about like clothes
Lovers had strewn in their desolate motel room

Out by the strip club that never cards teenage boys.
The snow is melting, and the snow is mush,
The snow is marked by oil stains; no thrush
Appears at your gate, or sings. You lean
Back, to try and open, with less-nimble fingers,
The buttons, bows, and taped-up vessels
Of love. It was given, it was received, it's gone.
The cold eventual evening whispers its nothing-song
And you and your Irish granny put the record on.

DECEMBER 2020

NEW GOLD DREAM, 21, 22, 23, 24...

I am going to the memory palace
To meet the Ice Queen and her fawns.
It dawns on me slowly, because
Dawns are slow, that this is now,
So memories have yet to come, are later,
So I am alone with the Queen of fear,
Who freezes me with her indifferent stare,
That looks beyond me, as if I was not there,
Which is not the case, I circle upon
The other circle in which she stands,
So there is a shared moment of Venn diagram,
But mostly we are in sets apart, as lacking
Hearts tend to be, in any logical entity, or two;
The nymphs and satyrs form a rowdy crew,
And they sip honey dew from lewd straws,
And in another world I might have rutted
With them among the golden burning hay,
As if this was Arcadia and I had all day
To be young, long-limbed, the next Bond,
But the air turns grey, and I am not blond,
Or fey, and this is a dawn that appears sunset
Now, in its revisited decline, for now I recall,
That to return to a remembered past is to die
Before being born, is to occur as a forethought,
Like a lost child on a movie lot, dark child star
Never to go super-nova; the novitiates spin
Their randy pastries on pink birthday plates,
And the goat-footed carnality bursts bubbles
That the blind pope puts out from his wee pipe;
It was never my plan to codify a formal style
While trying to curtail disorder with a pen

Borrowed from the rather rude Pan, conned
Into thinking the conning tower stays dry
After the wolfen submarine dives into the wild sea.
Captain of my one-man voyage, the poles above,
The undeciphered seabed below, I'm sandwich
For the Kraken, dryads and assorted mariners
Who never reached this sub-arctic realm of hers,
But now I disembark from a cage of steel that roars
With nuclear screws churning the waves, to locate
The perennial ark of all lovers, all poets, all fools,
The supreme architected compendium of things,
Where perfected maths of beauty beat mortal kings.
I have no more to do or say, I arrived to only leave,
But in the seeing that she declines to recognise
That only her image is icon of my lamplit eyes,
I fall a second time, or is that a third, from paradise,
Because without my Beatrice I am like Ulysses
When old and no longer moving on the spume,
A paralysed costume that once was action,
And this is death, or worse than that, I presume,
It is to become the afterimage of a heroic time,
When to have held her was the high mountain climb,
When to breathe was to starve for oxygen, yet thrill
At the rarest emptiness the hawk in blue absence
Achieves, at the mounting pinnacle just before
The furthest fastest dive-bombing down to kill.

JANUARY 2021

FOR THE EASTER OF 2021, IT MAY BE

What is coming will be good
But first we must wade in blood
To carry across the holy Rood,

Which is heavy but lightens in
The living bloodletting of the spring,
When all the flowers incarnate

The bodies that lift up from death,
Their petals bodacious insignia of
Christ's infirm fatality, strange love

That resists definition, unless sin
Is seeded at the tulip's core,
The rose's soul itself rotten,

As if a carnation could be evil
On day one – or is it that natural
Behaviour, from contagion to claw

Represents a sordid imagining
Of what perfection could only be
If designated to shape itself from clay?

The potter's insipid banalities the best
She could do, very much below par,
So creation is a demiurge's bargain

Basement knock-off of a designer's
Actual, for the catwalk, finer work?
It's possible the rack we take our bodies

From is shoddy piece trade, born
Of labour scantily paid, a scandal
In the heavens to please Pullman,

Whose comprehension of Man
And Superman is hardly Miltonic;
I consider atheists to be of the *Dunciad* –

God's not an absence to be described,
You cannot disprove the force of love –
Creation is, Crucifixion happened,

And Jesus dies daily in the Covid wards.
It's all one tumble, a monad, crushed
Together, like a sweets wrapper balled;

Angelic, or dire, the arch-fiend holds
A part of the final construct up, ungrammatical
Because incorrect, and disobedient.

It's a pent-up hullabaloo, a jailbreak rage,
So that on Easter's vile week of humiliations,
We see villains appear to play at tearing apart

The most gentle lamb that ever shed
Virgin wool to clad a babe; but it is art.
There's a lack of control when there should be,

And complications, drama and enemies,
Rises, descents, and turns of fortune to dizzy
The most addicted rider of amusement cars,

But in the Aristotelian end, after resolution,
The anti-climax is the anti-death, the bend
Of the river that suddenly comes clear,

When all expectant townsfolk,
With sun-scrambling fear, out-crowd
The edge, at sighting a peeling freighter
Grown in the eye, offering serum to the pier.

JANUARY 2021

THE IDYLLS OF THE FOOL – 5 SONNETS AND A CODA

Nothing is convenient, and there is never
A good time to be sacrificed to the gods
Of fame's indifferent gluttony. As
The epitome of the discardable,
I'm not for recycling, a wrapper
For a sweet invented by pacifists,
Now owned by war-makers.
I cavort in a high-ceilinged vacuum,
A dying king's court is barely ideal
For hijinks. Still, playful idolatries,
Sidelong glances, petty affairs
Pass the time between numb life
And a lavish funeral ceremony
That will bankrupt the next potentate.

This kingdom buries their entertainers
With the pharaoh, I'm date-stamped,
And due for a tomb without song.
Strumming my lyre, winking at a princess,
Few if any spy my misfortunes,
Being squat, secondary, an epiphenomenon.
You may think being a cut-up cut-rate
Trickster in motley is a good gig,
Complete with belled cap for a wig,
As I take innumerable swigs of mead,
Have little need for a new role,
But since my Ulysses lolls half-lifeless
On his carved marble throne
Like tyrant winter had come early to tie

The spring, let us sing of the decline
Of jolly times, and tropic climes,
For a moribund kingdom is un-droll.
Meanwhile, my gold pile is as much
Use as a eunuch in a queen-sized bed, how to
Buy back those days when I was fab?
The courtiers now are lean, drab, dull;
Useless work takes its toll. We
Should be sailing West, or wherever else
Risk sharpens its claws, seeking out laws
To test; we should be scaling crags
To perforate giant nests, to steal eggs
Golden, rare, unimaginably potent.
It is never too late to steal away,

When the tide is prepared to bear
The crew to illustrious vagabond days
Without bonded women, dreams or delay –
Days of riveted action, aroused with instant
Purpose, the rigor of having to do and be.
The having no time to think, just time to see
That what gets done is heroism defined.
Such journeying is uppermost in my mind
As I reflect on my liquidised, drifting, lord.
Oh, how I'd love to throw his piqued chains off,
And bundle him back onboard, for one final
Crazy feast at the high table of mythmaking seas!
Give me uncertain nights, unknown weeks,
To a long-expected peaked doom foretold,

Certain as school exams or witless lays.
The old bones of even magisterial kings creak,
But as his eyes meet mine over the cracked rim
Of his overwrought goblet, I can recognise
A signal, even now, to me, his first, best, bard –
Companion still, not gone are the glories –
His wink commands me to plan a last foray,
Hurrah for the escape that defeats death's doldrums,
We both flee to a future, as panjandrums undulate
To the banging of godless, lazy, imponderable drums.
Only disturb the play! Tear the costumes hard!
Aside, pigeons! Conventional hours obey idiocy.
It is a long madness we eagles choose to assay.
Art's more interesting if rules bend astray!

The sun is sinking nearby villainous behemoths,
A debatably divine abyss, fusing with an occult sigil
That glistens in half-light, lustrous chaos of beyond
What is purely earth-bound, further than testing oceans!

NEW SPRING POEM IN 33 COUPLETS

Spring is the word again.
Spring is a happening waiting

to accident. It surprises by always
showing up. Spring is your best lover,

the one you turn to in the night
to remember how good things can be.

Spring is the opposite of an ending.
Spring contains a spark plug, a paradox

and a big box of matches.
Spring dances drunk at a wedding

between the sky and earth.
Spring is every god at once.

Spring is the Shakespeare
of seasons. Spring votes

for the sun. Before spring
is only everything still to play for.

Spring does what it says
on the tin. Spring is an end

of the middle about to begin.
Spring wears a gold ring

on every wee finger. Spring owes
us money. Spring always pays

its debts. Spring is a reliable
witness. Spring is uncontrollable

science on the floor. Spring
is alive and kicking at the door.

Spring enters like a happy bear
driven wild by bountiful honey.

Spring drives a horse and carriage
through the crockery department

roaring horns and shaking tambourines.
Spring eats Tamburlaine for breakfast.

Spring rains cats and dogs and likes that.
Has a mind of spring. Spring

is mess, times four. Spring cleans
what others would leave behind.

Spring invented Mary Kondo.
Spring publishes good news only.

Spring has no sibling rivalry, okay?
It never springs but it pours.

Spring is a six-letter reverb.
Spring is louder than flowers.

Spring is suing sex for infringement
of copyright. Spring is as big

as London times infinity.
Spring is where all the fun occurs.

Spring was long before resurrection
or the sermon on the mount. Spring

helps winter to safely dismount.
Spring is pell-mell without pitstops.

Spring collides with chaos like a kiss.
Spring is impossible to avoid

and never missed. Spring is eponymous.
Spring sports an Easter bonnet

twice the size of noon. Spring sips
mid-day for afternoon tea. Spring loves

to play croquet on the lawn with bees
and birds and tinier slugs and such.

Spring considers you. Always will.
Spring precedes existence. Spring opens

up ambiguity like a shell. Spring obviates
the need for a living hell. Spring

knows Kora biblically. Spring inspired
the whole shebang. Spring is carbon neutral.

Spring is binary, open, multiple –
Spring means more more more.

'THIS IS THE POEM'

This is the poem with masks,
The poem with rain,
This is the one with delays,
Cancelled meetings,
Cold benches, empty parks,
This is the poem with less
Than desired, with excitement
Contained, barely, the poem
About keeping it bottled in,
About waiting forever,
This is the poem about love
That never explains itself,
That never gets revealed
At the end of the movie,
This is the poem about American
Diners, and waitresses chewing gum
That never meet the jet fighter pilot
And go off on the Harley,
This is the poem about soup
Without salt, and holidays
That disappeared one by one
Like in Agatha Christie,
This is the poem about swimming
Underwater for a whole year,
Holding your breath,
Waiting to surface, this is
The billionth poem about 2020
And 2021, also about Napoleon
Dying two hundred years ago
On an island, where he could not leave;

This is about history being a rainy day,
This is about great injustices,
And the small, local, meaningful moments
That never happen, between people
Who never meet, this is the poem
About trains speeding past,
And about masks being lifted slowly.

THE POST OFFICE
On The Bard's birthday – 8 Sonnets

You know the world has gone to Pol Pot
When the big news is The Post Office
Apologising for having falsely framed
Thirty-nine formerly disgraced Post-
Masters because a computer said to do it.
Actually, you know that already, when
People are dying for a lack of oxygen
In Delhi, Brazil, and parts of nations
In denial. I have to grimace at the pinnacle
We're edging off of, like an ASMR
Podcast reaching its naughty guardian
Angel conclusion at minute ten-thirty.
I feel dirty in stereo, but headphones
Keep getting smaller, you can conceal!
A True Crime vice, like an X-ray spy pen.
Thank Christ for Biden, I need to include

This guy in every new poem, he's saving
The planet. Waiting in the wings,
The other dude, the one who is lewd,
Rude and prepping for the mid-terms,
Because power's pendulum swings,
As Jim Rohn's podcast promises, It Can Turn!
He means, one day you are Cain or Abel.
Then the next day you are Cain or unable
To come to the phone right now,
Skull water-damaged by a flinty bone,
Or standstill stone. Keep waiting, the seasons
Will inevitably come around to the one
That yields wheat or oranges in the groves.
Luck, like medical charts, ups and downs.

Keep going, that is the message for the troops.
We were born to be duped, copied in
To the message that fires us from a gun.
Yesterday, we learned in World War One,
The British Empire decided not to bother
Putting the names on graves for anyone
Black, Brown, or in any other way inferior
To their idea of whiteness. Maybe Three
Hundred and fifty-thousand dead fighters
Lowered into the unfit pit, with only a bare
Stone rolled over the un-saluted ground,
Salting a century with ungrown respect;
Neglect is the stone that falls bloodied
From the brother's hand, leaves the other

Forgotten. I don't want history like that
Anymore, the whole shebang is rotten
To its self-satisfied core. I am locating
A pattern in the variants that keep coming
Around – first, the world has always been filled
With living struggle, before it was just ferns.
And you have to try to juggle fire on sticks,
Because if they fall, the sticks soon burn,
And not everyone gets their kicks
That way. Some of us persons
Are in the pay of a Colonel,
And we either sing, Elvis,
Stealing your culture,
Or we go to war. Both, in truth.

Today we heard on the news that cats
Can catch Covid-nineteen from me,
Basically, or any other feline fan;

I was an Egyptian in a previous priestly
Existence, shaved head, robes, and dust
From a sandstorm in my eyes, and a cat
I'd bow to, because not all religion is sane,
But mine was – who could worship a dog,
When a fine, lithe, enigmatic, likely to spring
Puss-in-boots can lick a paw with the éclat
Of Fred Astaire tap-dancing. The pussy's savoir
Faire is beyond compare, they compelled mice
To build the pyramids. Which continues the theme
For this show – you are either Tom or Jerry,

Japan or Captain Matthew C. Perry.
I am often self-referencing, possibly due
To an early failure to take up competitive fencing,
My only cut and thrust, dexterous riposte,
Must, by definition, take shape in verbal
Jousting – and so, lacking the wit to go out
And find another mind to debate with directly,
I work out my foul parliamentary tics in this box
Of laws, codes, benches and halls,
Poetry that elects its own self-serving rebels,
Voting for irregular line breaks, and para-
Rhyme, or enjambment for the poor.
I am a one nation Tory, and a ragamuffin
Without land, in the same electoral command –

None and all of this gerrymandered rambling
Across fenced-off property is planned – throw
Myself under the horses that seek the cunning fox!
It was Churchill who issued the edict
That non-white soldiers should not have individual
Marble after they gave the ultimate for King

And country, so Gary Oldman should give back
His Oscar for playing the old man as some noble
Moses with bifocals and a bathtub penchant.
It's not pleasant, but we're either the boot
Or the face, to get Orwell, or since this is Shakespeare's
Birthday, you're going to have to be or not be
The one with the poison-tipped rapier
At the end of the play when the villains

Either pile like an orgy gone horribly wrong,
Or the hero herself has their dying day,
For Ophelia floats down the years as the mirror
That deception, murder and politics raises high.
I am the one, the one, the one, the one, that lies
In state, or licks the broken plate, the ghost
At the banquet, the low-drowned at Morecombe Bay,
We are the treachery-blinded, the at sea lost,
The tempest-tossed, and only magic can rescue
Caliban, you can't win when sinned against is sinning,
And the most dramatic thing the pawns can do
Is cross the minefield and become a killing Queen.

APRIL 23, 2021

BORN TO BE WILD

Of the cold light of the cold light
One is struck
By being struck
By the theology
Of doublings,
The Jesus on the mount,
And the one on the cross,
The crossing guard,
And the one in the bar,
Which only makes sense

Or is legal
When one adds an afterwards.
History is consilience,
Or just negligent,
Or perhaps a heretic
With time on her hands.
Anyone else keep a few
Classics unread, unseen,
For the last days
Planning to be hooked

To the undying machine?
I would think you'd need to be
Husserl to really experience
What it's like for a girl,
Or boy; I say am bisexual,
Which is now as old hat
As a pratfall in a vaudeville hall.
Poems don't add up, you keep

Adding to them like geology,
They're incremental, fluvial,

Alluvial, elusive, allusive,
They can take more layers,
Like a cake evolving
Into a thesis on Kubrick
Or Ken Dryden, or Dick
DeBartolo or Kenneth Branagh,
Or that old hag in the poem by Frost,
Who scared the hell out of me.
Roberto had dark places he'd hide
In plain sight usually in white snow.

I know, I know.
Don't go, keep reading. Keep meeting
The next stage of my decline,
Which is yours, we go down together
But not like that. Conversation
Was Antin's thing, you can say
A poem should talk or be alphabetic,
Tick like a bomb, swing like an aristocat,
Take a dive like a bum boxer, or pray,
But that's opinion, backed up by guns

Or degrees or some forms of power,
Or you're just Vachel Lindsay, Keats,
Or any gal or guy who grew up in Vaudreuil.
Can't spell for beans anymore,
Thankfully don't have many beans
In these texts, and texts is such a dry word,
It hardly suggests the luminous landscape
Of the nimbus of these isles that soar...
It's sublime, it's rhetorical, it's propaganda
For a dud vaccine... prettiest ass I ever done saw

Was the one Jesus rode in on.
Gotcha, hey? Only the baby and the old wino
Survived, and all their blood is gone to dust...
Don't trust space missions. Don't trust devils
Selling you opium up the Yangtse.
The Tsetse kills, where is the cure for that?
Same as it ever was... we can predict
The next century – Russia, China, mars, wars,
Satellites, warming, AI, nanobots, covidiots,
More Netflix hits, opiates injected by eyeball,

And pornography in 4d; a fifth force
Smaller than a tiny invisible horse.
When Connery died, I thought, there goes a man
Who slapped women and starred in the best Bonds.
I held opposing ideas in my soul,
My intellection. If I am only meat, then
I am going to heat up and be ready soon.
Fear strikes out, and the diamonds are loaded.
I swerve between meanings like an obstacle course
Because being straight is too easy. I'm an asexual

Steer who likes attention and Chicago hot dogs.
The stakes are high, but they slope off pretty quickly.
Weave a circle in the fire, and admire
The spell makers who become their spells,
Like steelmakers pour the Bessemer of themselves
In the smelting ironworks. Either you're for Jesus,
Or Hegel, or Freud or Marx, or Einstein, or Joe Biden.
It's not allowed, anymore, to be hard or cruel,
Follow the golden rule. Return me, lover, to
A school of soft licks and sporting tricks,

If I was prime minister I'd bed a member of state.
I'd up the usual rate. Rhyme is as dumb as a pun
For the verbally misbehaving cheapskate.
You can change syntax, slip lexical field,
Go about your business with a high yield,
Veer across the patterns of signification,
But in the end, it's gonna be a staycation.
Shake appeal means a little bit of whirling hip,
A teeny-weeny bit of biting lip, a slap-happy

Honeygirl on VK, the party's in my trance,
You're all invited, except for NASA, they're already here!
The point of this loose exercise, this finger wag,
Is to imply that just getting drunk on flimsy
Whimsy can be a mighty fun way to spend
Your tongue coin, monsignor.
It's a churn that abates
Only when the maker makes the decision to designate
The line between frisson, division and spinning plates.
The circus is mastered by the clown in the middle

Of the lions and tigers, the Venus in spurs,
And the dizzying brothers up above us all,
In their silver apples and golden suns,
Flipping and slipping from limb to limb,
As if drawing a blueprint for calamity
Out of expert anatomy in decline and topple,
But inverted to achieve a mastery of a thing,
So, the Jesuit becomes a fool for a bird,
And I end up my enemy's loving dangling
Ding-a-ling. You're either führer or Paul's

Apostle in the spiritual tussle between angel and ego.
That's the final summation of this city of Todd –
You can bumble along just okay, but fame,
Adoration and corporeal success at the academy
Come with a connection to a network of techne.
Come blow my candles, devour my cake,
I only wanted to entertain you; I was only on the make.
Swap my dress for your cadet outfit, lipstick!
My lips. Fire all of your guns at once, and embrace
The way it all seems to be pointing to the fittest in space.

APRIL 8, 2021
CELEBRATING 40 YEARS OF WRITING POEMS

FOR SUETONIUS

these eternal
animals who do not know
their immediacy is limited
my cat Suetonius vivid black
on the snow-linked stones
completely emperor of garden
salute our creature fellows
establishing time as this now
their presence the beauty of
what there is to stretch or crawl
learn a languid solid stoic meow

CATHY'S CLOWN

'I die each night I hear this sound / here he comes that's Cathy's clown'

As the Anglican communion withers on the vine,
After centuries of Brexit-like post-papal decline,
Britain finds its new age built on a looser soil,

Belief brittle, online, feckless and vainly personal,
As if the idea of a higher being was a crass magic
That the Francis Crick 'team' had finally licked

With an ace crackerjack vaccine that mainly works
When it infuriates the French, Germans and Turks...
What other church is overseen by a former oil exec

Who admits to often being a bit depressed, atheistic?
It's difficult running a side-split faith organisation
Derived from a randy king's desire for penetration

In multiple ways not approved of by the testaments –
Only in England could 'bells and smells' be meant
In the best possible way, could priests be somewhat gay,

Yet told not to sleep together, in direct contrast, say,
To their founding tediously ruthless King Henry;
And yet, at Easter, even this motley, torn committee,

By definition mediocre, part-human, half-manticore,
Has to pause to reflect on the past four quarters,
And recognise that saving billions to shut vestry doors

Is a downbeat from love the meek, 'focus on' the poorest;
The trees have walked out of the forest, leaving a lone
Branch, on which waits a BAME uneducated allophone,

Who represents the structural flaws in every system,
For it is not our fault to sin; the seam leads to him –
We can unravel our corporate suits of tailored silk,

It does no harm, he cries to us, spilling graceful milk,
It's an anachronistic message that doesn't poll well,
It 'turns off' the Tory libertarian, the woke millennial –

No one wants to be told what to do, especially by a man
Claiming odd truths that don't hate on the Romans.
Pay your taxes, never judge a sexual deviant, or leper –

It's unpalatably kind, cowering, no lion, a low purr –
A belly rolled over, a shrug, a sort of giving up to higher
Laws, forces, another self or mind, as if to forgive liars,

As if to sue for peace, bury hatchets, let complaint go.
Not as if, that is what it is, a way to not become fixated credo
Above the moment's compassionate facts on the ground.

Which is why, after lifting to be bled out he made a sound,
A sad death-rattle, that slowly, silently, then louder still,
Broke half the world open as a boulder shifted uphill.

55 (X 2)

Nothing could have prepared me
For being born
In Montreal, not even the long
18th century, the little ice age,
Or the summer my father learned

To swim and dive. As stoics
Enjoy saying, ad nauseum,
Death is like thinking
Of all the years before birth.
It barely registers and cannot hurt.

What doesn't hurt doesn't make you
Exist, or their other idea, that earth
Mingles Caesar and commoner alike.
It's a strange comfort to be told
Your time preparing to arrive

Is what death is – so we come
From death; then birth is stealing
From the dead world? This is not
What I want to go on about
In this prattling meandering form

In which I choose to materialise
Before you, which is what poems are,
A way to teleport back and forth –
In time and space, the zoom call
Of their day. All early arts are replaced

Eventually by a better way to sing
Happy birthday or choose a hot date,
Or haggle over shares of some corporate
Entity, itself a metaphor. I was born
On Good Friday in Montreal,

Very small. The doctor told my parents
I would not survive the Easter holidays,
In all likelihood. How this was felt,
Or understood, I was told later.
I was placed in an incubator,

And my parents, in their twenties,
Were sore afraid. They looked at me
Like a warped and hairy monkey,
As small as a baby bird fallen out
Of some high nest. I survived,

And this was described, invariably,
As a miracle, which it was, since
Medicine was less advanced back then.
I don't feel any grateful surge
Towards the nurses, orderlies,

Or recall my mother's gloved rubber arm
Caressing my wrinkled, sapiens' brow.
Somehow, the before and after both remain
Beyond recall, nestled in the space
Some refer to as liminal – a threshold,

Where death and birth are as close as twins,
Neither subordinate to the other,
A sister and brother, curled up
In each other's arms, not tied to the other,
But not separate either, a perfect alliance,

And no one was any the wiser
As to which would slip back or away,
And whether birth or death
Would be the child they'd meet that day.
This is fanciful, a narrative arc;

Is there a life spark? A moment, a bang?
We know there is conception, or is that, also
Just a myth of science? Contact happens,
It has to, for various materials to coalesce.
Items in a basket jostle, never fuse,

But life is made from molecules that care
Enough about connection to go the extra mile;
But it is probably all automatic, not driven
By a passionate thought. How could it not be,
Though? In some deep smallest place,

That some contorted collider will soon uncover,
Might there be a monkey tinier than me, even,
The fuse we mention in poetry, moving
Planets, flowers, light and love? Dante
Wanted to locate this tiniest factor in love itself,

So love moves love, and love revolves, as love
Too evolves, into a later amalgamation.
I am confused, because I am speaking from
The moment of least knowledge, the ledge
Of the shelf, the interior that is outside, barely.

It's embarrassing, so intimate, but you could say
Remote. Going back to more homely facts,
My father had a beard, and
Looked like Fidel Castro. My mom drove
A red sportscar, had a beehive hairdo *(entre acte)*.

It was baseball season or would be. In a year Expo
'67 would see the geodesic dome of Buckminster
Fuller built close to our home;
What would be our home, six years later;
The jumble of pieces of a story

That fades constantly, as I think more and more
On what it could mean to have gratitude
For existence. Do I thank lust, desire, divinity?
A gentle embrace that went too far in that red car?
No judgment, but I managed to get more years

Than some emperors, some empires.
Birth never requires an equal magnitude to impress,
We would be blessed however long we endured,
We never know the span to come,
We start across a bridge being built, that finishes

Off into the fog, incomplete, without a sense of
If Isambard Kingdom Brunel engineered it –
None of this is that day, the careful placing of my body
By some unknown medical worker, at the General
Hospital, into the plastic, or glass, receptacle, to keep

That tremulous still-growing creature in motion.
I do not think of the commotion in the disturbed air,
The motes in the bars of sun, any more than I remember
How Brutus saw his blade shine like a porpoise in water
Before he decided to end a tyranny to create a new war.

GOOD FRIDAY 2021

BIO NOTE

Todd Swift is the author of over two dozen poetry collections, from pamphlets, to full collections, and his poems have appeared in many newspapers, anthologies, and journals, around the world. He was recently visiting scholar at Pembroke College, Cambridge, as poet in residence for a year. With a PhD in modern poetic style from UEA, where his supervisors included Jon Cook and Denise Riley, he has taught poetry, screenwriting, and theory at universities in the UK and Hungary. He was born in Montreal, Quebec, Canada, on Good Friday, in 1966, and misses making snow forts and jumping into lakes in July. He has a godson, Alex, and many nieces and nephews. His favourite cat is Suetonius. He is director of the Black Spring Press Group, founded in 1985. In 2019 he came third place in the election for Oxford Professor of Poetry. In 2013 he became both British and Catholic. He is married to an Irish barrister.